Supers

Maserati

Robert Walker

🌱 **Crabtree Publishing Company**

www.crabtreebooks.com

Superstar Cars

Author: Robert Walker
Publishing plan research and development:
 Sean Charlebois, Reagan Miller
 Crabtree Publishing Company
Editors: Sonya Newland, Adrianna Morganelli
Proofreader: Molly Aloian
Editorial director: Kathy Middleton
Project coordinator and prepress technician: Ken Wright
Print coordinator: Katherine Berti
Series consultant: Petrina Gentile
Cover design: Ken Wright
Design: Simon Borrough
Photo research: Sonya Newland

Produced for Crabtree Publishing by
White-Thomson Publishing
Photographs:

F. Jack Jackson: p. 12; Tony Wilson-Bligh: p. 41; David
Chedgy: p. 42-43; CuboImages: p. 50-51. **Corbis:** Geneviève
Chauvel/Sygma: p. 28; Bettmann: p. 29; Michael Cole: pp.
46-47; Car Culture: p. 44-45. **Dreamstime:** Hupeng: p. 7;
Lorenzo Dottorini: p. 32-33. **Flickr/Creative Commons
License:** Ciccio Pizzettaro: p. 2, 10-11; Jano2106: p. 38-39; Rex
Gray: p. 47; Jez B: p. 52-53; George Perfect: p. 58-59. **Getty
Images:** p. 16; Gamma-Rapho: p. 8-9; SSPL: p. 13; AFP: p. 30;
Popperfoto: p. 40. **Motoring Picture Library:** p. 4, 6, 8, 34-35,
49; Tom Wood: p. 21, 24, 26-27. **Shutterstock:** samotrebizan:
cover (background); Jemny: p. 1, 4–5, 55; Rui Ferreira: p. 17;
Adriano Castelli: p. 18; Massimiliano Lamagna: p. 36; Stefan
Ataman: p. 37; ermess: p. 48; Ferenc Szelepcsenyi: p. 54-55;
EvrenKalinbacak: p. 56; Zoran Karapancev: cover (car), p. 57;
KENCKOphotography: p. 59. **Wikipedia/ Creative Commons
License:** thesupermat: p. 14-15; Brian Snelson: p. 19, 25;
Detectandpreserve: p. 20; Tony Harrison: p. 22; Craig Howell:
p. 23; Lucas P/GNU Free Documentation Licence: p. 30-31;
AlfvanBeem: p. 43, 52.

Library and Archives Canada Cataloguing in Publication

Walker, Robert, 1980-
 Maserati / Robert Walker.

(Superstar cars)
Includes index.
Issued also in electronic formats.
ISBN 978-0-7787-2102-4 (bound).--ISBN 978-0-7787-2107-9 (pbk.)

 1. Maserati automobiles--Juvenile literature. I. Title.
II. Series: Superstar cars

TL215.M34W34 2012   j629.222'2   C2012-902285-3

Library of Congress Cataloging-in-Publication Data

CIP available at Library of Congress

Crabtree Publishing Company

www.crabtreebooks.com   1-800-387-7650

Printed in the U.S.A./052012/FA20120413

Published in Canada
Crabtree Publishing
616 Welland Ave.
St. Catharines, Ontario
L2M 5V6

Published in the United States
Crabtree Publishing
PMB 59051
350 Fifth Avenue, 59th Floor
New York, New York 10118

Published in the United Kingdom
Crabtree Publishing
Maritime House
Basin Road North, Hove
BN41 1WR

Published in Australia
Crabtree Publishing
3 Charles Street
Coburg North
VIC 3058

>> Contents

Chapter 1
The House of the Trident »»»

If Maserati could be summed up in one word, it would be "speed." Carlo Maserati first laid his hands on an engine more than 100 years ago and since then, the family name has been synonymous with excellence under the hood. From its humble beginnings, the Italian carmaker has carved out its place among the world's top racing and road automobiles.

Going places fast

Maserati's accomplishments have not been limited to engines. Its innovations in body design have produced some of the most recognizable models in the world. Cars such as the Birdcage and the 250F have helped Maserati to many victories under its own banner, as well as for other teams.

The Birdcage, or Tipo 60, earned its nickname for its cage-like **chassis**.

A little Italian

The Italian word "tipo" has appeared in the name of Maserati cars since the company began producing vehicles over 80 years ago. Tipo means "type" in English. It is used along with a number to indicate a new model and distinguish it from the previous one. This practice was used by many Italian automakers.

A Maserati car in the lead is a common sight on race-tracks around the world.

A recipe for success

Maserati's **longevity** is due to its combination of innovation and determination. Top designers work tirelessly to plan and perfect the next generation of Maserati cars. A state-of-the-art production line builds them. And when it comes to the racetrack, Maserati's roster of talented drivers and race teams blow past the competition.

Against all odds

Even with all the winning pieces in place, it has not been an easy road for Maserati. Competition in the sports car industry is fierce. Big names such as Ferrari, Jaguar, and Lamborghini are just a few of the giants Maserati has had to go up against. There have also been financial difficulties for Maserati, and the company has changed hands several times. Even with all these obstacles, Maserati persevered and has not only survived, but succeeded.

5

≫ The Brothers Maserati

The Maserati family lived in the small Italian town of Voghera, Lombardy. Carlo was the eldest son, followed by Bindo, Alfieri, Mario, Ettore, and Ernesto. Their father was a railroad engineer, and the Maserati children had a love of machines from an early age.

A need for speed

By the early 1900s, Carlo had begun working at a bicycle factory. Not satisfied with pedal power, Carlo constructed a single-**cylinder** engine that could be fixed to a bicycle. With a little work and a few false starts, Carlo soon had his contraption up and running. He began entering the motorized velocipede in local races, blowing away the competition. Carlo even set a land-speed record with a time of almost 31 mph (50 km/h).

Carlo Maserati (right) began his career working at a bicycle factory. He was soon converting pedal bikes into engine-powered machines.

The Maserati logo

The Maserati badge is a three-pointed spear called a trident. It was designed by Mario Maserati. The idea came from a statue of Neptune, the Roman god of the sea, that stands in Bologna, Italy. Bologna was the site of the first Maserati headquarters. Maserati earned the nickname "House of the Trident" from Mario's design.

Hungry for more speed, Carlo went to work for the Italian company Isotta Fraschini. A renowned maker of engines for cars and planes, Isotta Fraschini was also responsible for designing one of the first all-wheel braking systems.

Learning the ropes

Carlo was able to get Alfieri a job at Isotta Fraschini, and they were soon joined by Bindo and Ettore. Young Alfieri was only 16 at the time, but it did not take long for him to impress the company's owners.

Alfieri showed promise not only as a mechanic but behind the wheel as well. By 1908, he had earned a chance to race professionally for Isotta Fraschini. The talented young driver overcame engine troubles to finish fourteenth in his very first Grand Prix race.

The now **iconic** Maserati logo was inspired by the trident symbol of Bologna, the company's first home.

7

The birth of Maserati

Riding high on his success with Isotta Fraschini, Alfieri decided it was time for the Maserati brothers to go into business for themselves. In 1914, the doors opened at the Societa Anonima Officine Alfieri Maserati. They started out building fast racing cars and engines for other companies. Customers included former Maserati brothers' employers Isotta Fraschini and carmaker Diatto. Maserati also began making **spark plugs**, brakes, and **cylinder blocks**.

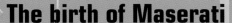

As good behind the wheel as he was under the hood, Alfieri led Maserati to some of its earliest successes.

Isotta Fraschini

The Societa Anonima Fabbrica di Automobili Isotta Fraschini began making engines in 1903. It was one of the first automotive manufacturers to produce cars with four-wheel brakes. The company still exists today, making engines for cars, boats, and airplanes.

The Tipo 26 was the first all-Maserati racer produced by the company.

Alfieri takes the wheel

Alfieri continued to develop as a driver, winning several important competitions. He took first at the Susa-Moncenisio in a car of his own design, as well as winning the Mugello Circuit and the San Sebastiano Grand Prix. Things were going well for Alfieri—until he was banned from racing.

A new focus

During a race, Alfieri had switched out his car's engine for a more powerful one in order to get up a steep hill. He was caught by racing officials, disqualified from the race, and banned from competitive racing for several years. But the determined Alfieri used his time away from the track to focus all his energies on creating the first car to bear the Maserati logo—the Tipo 26.

Vital Statistics

Tipo 26

Production years: 1926–32
No. built: 10
Top speed: 124 mph (200 km/h)
Engine type: Inline 8
Engine size: 1492 cc (1.5 liters), 128 bhp
Cylinders: 8
Transmission: 4-speed manual
CO_2 emissions: N/A
EPA fuel economy ratings: N/A
Price: N/A

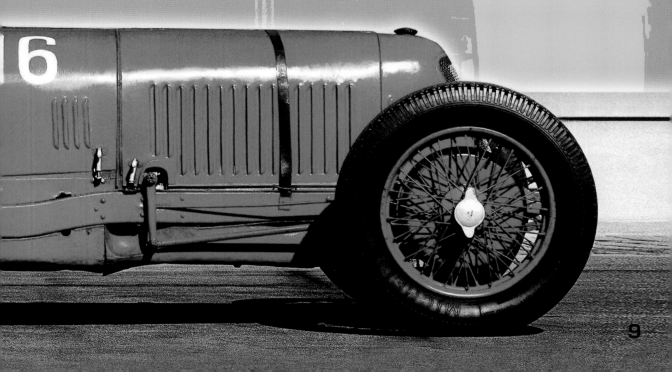

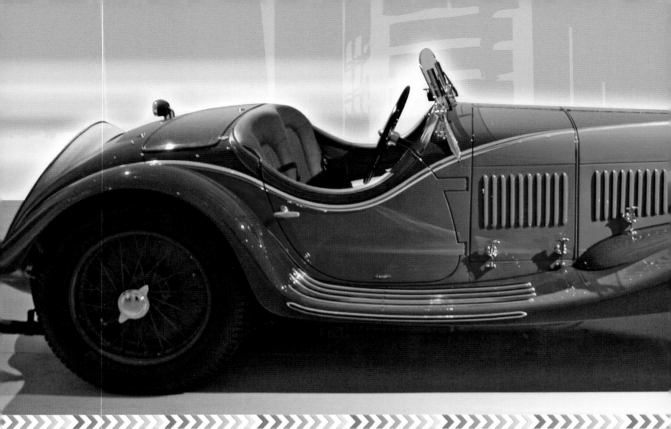

Winning from the start

The Tipo 26 was a two-seater racecar. It came with a powerful eight-cylinder, **supercharged** engine.

The Tipo 26 made its first appearance at the 1926 Targa Florio. The Targa Florio was one of the toughest endurance races at the time, with a 45-mile (72-km) route that weaved along the narrow mountain roads of Sicily, Italy.

Despite the demanding course, with Alfieri himself in the driver's seat the new Tipo 26 took first place.

 The Tipo V4 was as big as it was fast, weighing over 2,300 lb (1,043 kg).

Later successes

The following season, Alfieri took the next Tipo version, the 26B, to another impressive showing at the Targa Florio. The 26B's engine was increased to two liters, 155 **brake horsepower (bhp)**, with a top speed of almost 130 mph (210 km/h). It also went on to win the Italian Constructors' Championship and the Tripoli Grand Prix.

Early racing

Competitive racing today is very dangerous—but in the early 1900s it was even more so! Many races were held on public roads and highways instead of private racetracks. Also, drivers had much less protection than they do today. More focus was put on speed and performance than it was on keeping the driver safe.

The Tipo V4

The V4 came next, in 1929. The giant 16-cylinder engine was the combination of two Tipo 26B engines. Alfieri set a lap speed record with the V4 at the 1929 Monza Grand Prix, reaching almost 125 mph (201 km/h). His feat remained unbeaten for over 20 years. The V4 also set a Class C speed world record later that year, going over 153 mph (246 km/h).

The Tipo V4 went on to win the 1930 Grand Prix in Tripoli, as well as the Rome Grand Prix the following year. These successes were a huge windfall for Maserati, helping bring in the funds and acclaim that allowed it to boost its operations.

Chapter 2

Life After Alfieri ≫≫≫

Maserati said a sad goodbye to its founder in 1932. Alfieri died after undergoing an operation to try and repair some of the injuries he had received while racing. His death not only affected the Maserati family, but the racing world as well. Alfieri's funeral was attended by employees, admirers, and former competitors.

Alfieri's legacy

Back at the Maserati company, the remaining brothers—Ettore, Ernesto, and Bindo— pressed on. They continued with the designs Alfieri had been working on at the time of his death, including the 8C 2500. This was considered by many to be Alfieri's masterpiece, and proved to be a hit on and off the track. The road version came with a two- or four-seater open-top body, and boasted a top speed of almost 143 mph (230 km/h). The racer brought home several Grand Prix wins at Rome, Spain, and Monza.

Vital Statistics

8C 2500

Production years: 1930–32
No. built: 14
Top speed: 143 mph (230 km/h)
Engine type: Inline 8
Engine size: 2495 cc (2.5 liters), 185 bhp
Cylinders: 8
Transmission: 4-speed manual
CO_2 emissions: N/A
EPA fuel economy ratings: N/A
Price: N/A

The 8C 2500, or Tipo 26M, was a two-seater racing car.

NPX 126

! Alfieri's memory was kept alive as cars of his design won on the track. Car number 20 here is the Maserati 8C on the starting grid at the 1934 German Grand Prix.

Enter Adolfo Orsi

The Maserati brothers were excellent mechanics, but they were not the best businessmen. The company was growing, but there were financial worries, and the future of Maserati seemed uncertain. Around this time, Maserati came to the attention of successful Italian **industrialist** Adolfo Orsi, who bought shares in the company. Ettore, Ernesto, and Bindo remained in charge of designing and building cars. Orsi took control of the company.

The French marathon

The Le Mans 24 Hours race in France is one of the most difficult competitions in the world. Begun in 1923, Le Mans is an endurance race, with competitors driving day and night for 24 hours straight. Each team has two drivers, who take turns behind the wheel while the other driver rests.

War in Europe

In 1939, Maserati moved from Bologna to its present-day home in Modena, Italy. The Orsi company had a factory there. World War II broke out the same year, and Italy joined the fighting in 1940. Soon, carmakers turned their focus toward making vehicles and machinery to aid the war effort. Even though the war pretty much brought motor racing to a halt, the Maserati brothers continued to work on designs for future racing and road cars. The late 1930s had seen an increased threat from competing manufacturers on the track, and Maserati needed to find a way of staying ahead of the competition. This included plans for a racer with a supercharged six-cylinder engine.

The A6 1500 was the first Maserati car off the production line following the end of World War II.

The A6 1500 is unveiled

The war ended in 1945, and the Maserati brothers immediately returned to car production. At the 1947 Geneva Motor Show, they unveiled the A6 1500. This became Maserati's first production series road vehicle. The push for a sports car for everyday use came from Orsi, who wanted to expand the Maserati name beyond the racetrack.

A sports car for all

Planning and testing of the A6 1500 had begun as far back as 1941. The first test model was a two-seater **coupe**. Some small changes were made when the car went into production in 1947. These included the addition of two smaller back seats to accommodate passengers. While the A6 1500 was a hit with the public, it signaled the impending end of the Maserati family's involvement with the company that bore its name.

Maserati motorcycles

Most car enthusiasts would be surprised to learn about motorcycles bearing the Maserati name. While Maserati never actually made any bikes, their one-time owner Orsi also owned a motorcycle manufacturing company. This allowed for the use of the Maserati name and trident logo on a short-lived series of motorcycles.

The end of an era

The ten-year contract the Maserati brothers had signed when they sold control of Maserati to Orsi was coming to an end. Designer Alberto Massimino, who had joined the company in 1939, was given greater creative control. Maserati was enjoying a post-war boom, but it looked like Ernesto, Ettore, and Bindo would not be around to see it.

The Maserati brothers said goodbye to the company at the end of 1947. They returned to Bologna, along with a number of workers who remained loyal to the Maserati family. The three brothers opened a new factory, called the Officine Specializate Costruzioni Automobili (OSCA). They continued to make cars until the mid-1960s.

After Maserati

After leaving the company Alfieri had started, the Maserati brothers opened up a new automaking business near their former Bologna plant. Within a year, the small factory was up and running, entering the Circuito di Pescara, and winning at the Grand Prix in Naples in 1948. The company was sold to the Agusta family in 1963.

In the post-war years, a group of talented new drivers was added to Maserati's Grand Prix roster, including Stirling Moss.

250F

Production years: 1954–58
No. built: 26
Top speed: 180 mph (290 km/h)
Engine type: Inline 6
Engine size: 2493 cc (2.5 liters),
    240 bhp
Cylinders: 6
Transmission: 4-speed manual
CO_2 emissions: N/A
EPA fuel economy ratings: N/A
Price: N/A

With its fins and gill-like vents across its body, many thought the 250F looked like a shark.

Fierce competition

The post-war racing scene proved challenging for Maserati. Competitors such as Ferrari came out with faster, more powerful cars. At the start of the 1950s, Maserati found itself looking to reclaim its former place as a frontrunner in automotive racing. Gioacchino Colombo took control of design at Maserati in 1952, working to improve the A6G CM racer.

The 250F

Perhaps the most important Maserati car of this era was the 250F, a front-engined Formula 1 car that was in part inspired by the A6G CM. This now-classic racer brought home many important Grand Prix wins for Maserati during its lifetime, including four in 1957 alone. Several different versions of the 250F were produced between 1954 and 1958.

17

Off track

The 250F enjoyed great Formula 1 success, so it was a surprise when Maserati announced the end of its racing team in the late 1950s. Orsi had decided to focus on road cars instead. However, the company continued to design and build cars and engines for other racing teams.

On the road

This change in direction led to the creation of the Maserati 3500 GT (**grand tourer**), which came in both coupe and convertible styles. The four-seater featured the first Maserati engine produced exclusively for road cars. It combined comfort and handling for everyday use with a speed that appealed to the more adventurous driver.

A new design

The Tipo 60 is one of the most recognizable Maserati cars ever produced. It earned its nickname of "Birdcage" from its revolutionary framework—a complex series of crisscrossing steel tubes.

Designed by Giulio Alfieri, the Birdcage was born out of a need for a frame that was lightweight and sturdy. The Birdcage's engine was also as light as it was powerful, with a top speed of almost 168 mph (270 km/h).

The 3500 GT was a big hit among Hollywood celebrities and even royalty. Its popularity helped Maserati change its image from racing cars to road vehicles.

The racing Birdcage

The Tipo 60 was followed by another model in the series, the Tipo 61, which came with a larger engine for racing competitions in North America. Unfortunately, the placement of the engine at the front of the vehicle clashed with the growing trend for mid- and rear-engined racers. The new Birdcage had a relatively short lifespan on the racetrack, and only 16 cars were made.

Tipo 60

Production years: 1959–60
No. built: 21
Top speed: 168 mph (270 km/h)
Engine type: Inline 4
Engine size: 1990 cc (2 liters), 200 bhp
Cylinders: 4
Transmission: 5-speed manual
CO_2 emissions: N/A
EPA fuel economy ratings: N/A
Price: N/A

A brand new Birdcage

To celebrate the Birdcage's 75th anniversary, Italian designer Pininfarina built a new version called the Birdcage 75 in 2005. This *concept car* was a futuristic-looking re-imagining of the classic Maserati design. It had a bubble canopy that lifted up to allow the driver and passenger to enter and exit the vehicle.

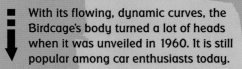

With its flowing, dynamic curves, the Birdcage's body turned a lot of heads when it was unveiled in 1960. It is still popular among car enthusiasts today.

New directions

The Maserati Sebring was launched in 1963. It was sold in North America as well as Europe, with the intention of spreading the Maserati name worldwide. Many design features were carried over from the previous 3500 GTI, such as the **suspension** and brakes.

The first series sold modestly. It had to go up against other new, more powerful models from manufacturers including Aston Martin. This led Maserati to come up with ways to match and surpass the competition, with the launch of the Sebring II and the Mistral.

New features from Maserati for the Sebring included air conditioning and an automatic transmission.

The winds of change

Named after a breeze that blows into the Mediterranean Sea in the winter months, the Mistral was anything but cold. It had a sleek body, a top speed of 155 mph (255 km/h), and it came in coupe and **spyder** versions. Less than a year into production, the engine was increased from 3.5 to 4.0 liters.

Later improvements

The Mistral would be the last of Maserati's classic six-cylinder GTs. There were no back seats for passengers, and it came with a **manual transmission** with the option for automatic. The second Sebring was an improvement on its predecessor, but the Mistral outsold it by twice the number. By the time production ended in 1970, over 828 coupe and 100 spyder versions of the Mistral had been sold.

The traditional grille on the Mistral was replaced with its air intake located under the front bumper.

Mistral

Production years: 1963–70
No. built: 928
Top speed: 155 mph (255 km/h)
Engine type: straight 6
Engine size: 3694 cc (3.5 liters), 245 bhp
Cylinders: 6
Transmission: 5-speed manual
CO_2 emissions: N/A
EPA fuel economy ratings: N/A
Price: US$13,000 (1963)

Meet the four-door

As well as the Sebring and Mistral, 1963 was also the year that Maserati launched its first four-door **sedan**, the Quattroporte (literally "four doors" in Italian). This was designed by Pininfarina, which for the last 50 years had worked for one of Maserati's biggest competitors—Ferarri. Thanks largely to its brand new V8 engine, which gave it a decent speed, the Quattroporte enjoyed modest success on the market. Production ran until 1969, and around 772 of the cars were built.

Selling out

In 1968, the Orsi family sold Maserati to the French automaker Citroën. The new owners brought Maserati increased financial security as well as

The Quattroporte quickly gained a reputation for being the fastest four-door sedan on the road, with a top speed of 144 mph (230 km/h).

sales potential, allowing for further growth and development in the company. As part of the sale, Maserati agreed to build Citroën's designs for the Bora and the Merak.

The next stage

The Quattroporte II, not released until 1974, featured a V6, 2965-cc Citroën engine. It was heavily based on Citroën designs, including its suspension and cabin design. This version was not very popular—customers wanted something more powerful than a V6. It turned out to be the last Citroën-owned Maserati car. By 1975, only 13 had been produced.

The Quattroporte III

The series finally hit its stride with the Quattroporte III in 1978, which returned to the spirit of the original Quattroporte. It came with a powerful V8, 4.2-liter engine, with an automatic transmission. The changes proved successful, and production of the Quattroporte III series continued until 1990. It included the 4.2, 4.9, and Royale versions.

The luxurious interior of a Quattroporte III. The car was so popular that even then-Italian president, Sandro Pertini, owned one.

Mid-engine design

The Bora series was the first mid-engine design for Maserati sports cars. Launched in 1971, it featured a V8 engine with a top speed of almost 160 mph (257 km/h). This was another Citroën-led creation, designed to expand Maserati sales in North America, where it was sold with a larger version of the V8 engine. It underwent several adjustments to meet stricter emissions and safety requirements. The Bora was designed by Giorgetto Giugiaro and came in the 4.7 and 4.9 versions.

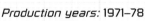

Vital Statistics

Bora 4.7

Production years: 1971–78
No. built: 289
Top speed: 174 mph (280 km/h)
Engine type: 90-degree V8
Engine size: 4719 cc (4.7 liters), 310 bhp
Cylinders: 8
Transmission: ZF 5-speed
CO_2 emissions: N/A
EPA fuel economy ratings: N/A
Price: US$25,000 (1971)

Standard features for the Maserati Bora included air conditioning and electric windows.

AMAGING FACTS ⚑

Bora name

Like the Mistral before it, the Bora took its name from a European wind. The bora is a cold northeasterly breeze that blows inland from the Adriatic Sea.

The Merak was known for having great response and control, and had a top speed of 149 mph (240 km/h).

A lighter Bora

Intended as a "junior" version of the Bora, and also designed by Giugiaro, the 1972 Maserati Merak was created to compete with similar models by its competitors. The Merak came with a V6 mid-engine, with 190 bhp. It offered more interior space than the competition, if not the same speed and power. When Citroën left Maserati in 1975, the new company owners came out with a more powerful version, the Merak SS, which offered 220 bhp.

Giorgetto Giugiaro

Italian designer Giorgetto Giugiaro had worked with big names such as Fiat and Alfa Romeo before coming to Maserati. He would form ItalDesign Giugiaro in 1967, which designed the very popular Volkswagen Golf. Today, ItalDesign Giugiaro designs boats and trains, as well as cars.

Chapter 3
Trouble for Maserati ⟫⟫⟫

The Orsi family sold its control of Maserati to Citroën in 1968. Since taking over in the late 1930s, the Orsis had experienced their share of highs and lows. During and after the war, Maserati had been successful in producing parts and machines, but even this proved difficult.

A rocky relationship

The Orsis had enjoyed a profitable business relationship with the country of Argentina. However, when Argentinean dictator Juan Perón was overthrown in 1955, a huge machine tools contract disappeared as well. Maserati suffered a million-dollar loss as a result of this political event. This played a big part in the family's decision to focus on the production of road cars.

Sales worries

There were also concerns about sales. Maseratis had been selling, thanks to designs such as the 3500 GT and the Quattroporte, but never in the kinds of numbers that Orsi had hoped for. Some estimates place the total of Maserati **production car** sales at less than 6,000 between the end of World War II and 1968.

Citroën

The French automaker Citroën was founded in 1919 by Andre Gustave Citroën. It would become one of the largest car manufacturers in the world within a decade of opening its doors. Citroën was the first European car company to mass-produce vehicles. This method of production was different from that used by most European carmakers at the time, which built luxury vehicles in relatively small numbers.

Citroën buys in

The Citroën-Maserati connection began in 1967, when the French automaker approached Maserati to help evolve its own DS Sport series. The intention was to combine the body and styling of Citroën with the power of a Maserati engine—the result was the Citroën SM. The relationship was beneficial to both companies. Citroën got the legendary engine-maker's abilities, and Maserati gained the funds it needed to develop its new V6 engine.

With the Orsis looking to sell and Citroën enjoying the success of its new SM, it seemed natural that the automaker would take over Maserati. But a series of events would soon turn the decision sour, and Maserati would face some of the darkest years in its history.

The Maserati-powered Citroën SM was a combination of French style and Italian power.

27

The Yom Kippur War

On October 6, 1976, several Arab nations attacked the country of Israel. The assault took place on Yom Kippur, a very important holiday in the Jewish religion. Known as a day of atonement, Yom Kippur is when Jewish people pray for forgiveness for anything they have done wrong in the past year.

Because it was a national holiday, businesses were closed and most people were at home—including a lot of Israel's soldiers.

After the attack, fighting lasted several weeks. The invading Arab nations were eventually defeated, at a cost of almost 2,700 Israeli lives. Although the fighting took place in Israel, the repercussions of the conflict would be felt around the world.

The Arab nations that invaded Israel were looking to reclaim former lands they had lost to Israel in previous conflicts.

During the oil crisis, the price of gas rose and availability dropped. People found it difficult to afford to drive their cars, even if they could get hold of gas.

OPEC's reaction

Many of the Arab nations involved in the Yom Kippur War were members of the Organization of Petroleum Exporting Countries (OPEC). These countries produce the majority of the world's oil. After the Yom Kippur War, they raised the price of oil. The Arab members convinced OPEC to put an **embargo** on the supply of oil to countries that supported Israel.

The oil crisis

As a result of the oil shortage, the price of gasoline skyrocketed. While the public felt the hit at the pumps, the auto industry felt it at the dealerships. With gas so expensive, people were no longer buying cars in the numbers they had before the crisis. Already worried about declining sales, the Citroën-owned Maserati had its troubles doubled. The future of the company was uncertain.

The end of Maserati?

Citroën's financial problems led to the sale of the company to French automaker Peugeot. Peugeot wanted to unload the troubled Maserati branch, and considered **liquidating** the company. Maserati would be broken up and sold. Hundreds of men and women employed by Maserati would be out of work.

The potential loss of all those jobs led a government agency to step in. The GEPI is a state-owned financial company that helps keep people employed. This organization took control of the struggling company. But it was a man from Maserati's past who really helped turn things around.

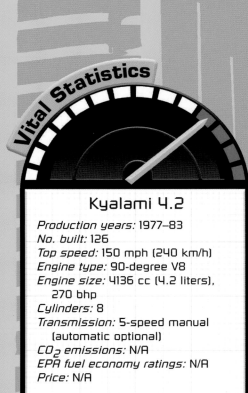

Vital Statistics

Kyalami 4.2

Production years: 1977–83
No. built: 126
Top speed: 150 mph (240 km/h)
Engine type: 90-degree V8
Engine size: 4136 cc (4.2 liters), 270 bhp
Cylinders: 8
Transmission: 5-speed manual (automatic optional)
CO_2 emissions: N/A
EPA fuel economy ratings: N/A
Price: N/A

Alejandro De Tomaso (right) was an Argentinean racing driver who had a Formula 1 career before turning to automaking.

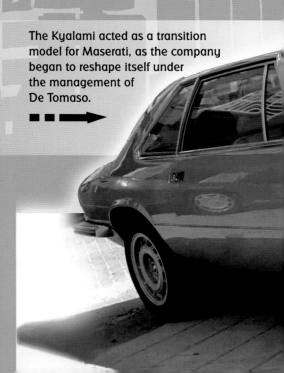

The Kyalami acted as a transition model for Maserati, as the company began to reshape itself under the management of De Tomaso.

Alejandro saves the day!

Alejandro De Tomaso was a former Maserati racecar driver who had formed his own company in 1959. In 1967, De Tomaso Automobili released the Mangusta. Constructed in a partnership with American auto giant Ford, the Mangusta proved to be a success. It was De Tomaso who arranged to take over control of Maserati from the government in 1975.

The Kyalami

It took a lot of work, but De Tomaso managed to bring the company back from the brink of disaster. He first oversaw the release of the Maserati Kyalami. A four-seater coupe, the Kyalami had a top speed of 150 mph (240 km/h). The model was a modest success, and allowed the company to release the now-legendary Quattroporte III. Sales slowly began to climb as Maserati entered the 1980s—a decade that would see the release of a brand-new style of car for the company.

Name tracking

The Maserati Kyalami model took its name from a racetrack in South Africa. Located near the city of Johannesburg, the Kyalami track played host to many South African Grand Prix competitions. In the 1980s, the track fell out of popularity with the racing world. Kyalami underwent major renovations in the 1990s and is now used once again to host major competitive events.

Maserati in the 1980s

De Tomaso's Maseratis of the 1980s moved from being mid-engine sports cars to more affordable front-engine coupes. Some people criticized what was considered a step down for the Maserati name, but overall the change was well-received by car enthusiasts and critics.

Bring on the Biturbo

The first Biturbo series was produced between 1981 and 1985. It marked the return of Maserati to the two-liter class, and featured a 90-degree V6 engine with twin **turbochargers**—a first for a road car.

The first Biturbo series was designed by Pierangelo Andreani, who worked with Pininfarina before coming to De Tomaso Maserati.

A boost for Maserati

Another innovation for the Biturbo was the introduction of the Maserati Automatic Boost Control system (MABC). This controlled the turbocharger boost pressure electronically. Produced into the 1990s, more than 30 different versions of the Biturbo were made.

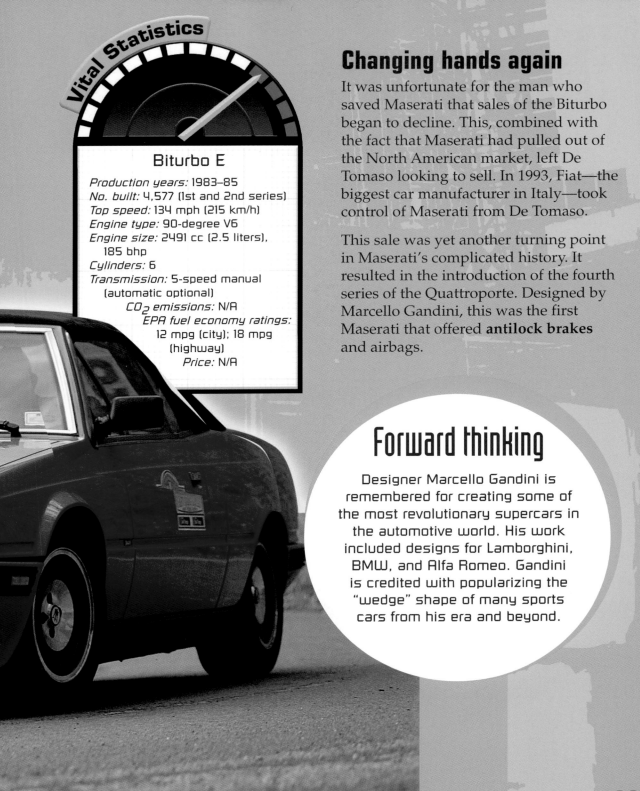

Biturbo E

Production years: 1983–85
No. built: 4,577 (1st and 2nd series)
Top speed: 134 mph (215 km/h)
Engine type: 90-degree V6
Engine size: 2491 cc (2.5 liters),
  185 bhp
Cylinders: 6
Transmission: 5-speed manual
  (automatic optional)
    CO_2 *emissions:* N/A
      EPA fuel economy ratings:
      12 mpg (city); 18 mpg
      (highway)
        Price: N/A

Changing hands again

It was unfortunate for the man who saved Maserati that sales of the Biturbo began to decline. This, combined with the fact that Maserati had pulled out of the North American market, left De Tomaso looking to sell. In 1993, Fiat—the biggest car manufacturer in Italy—took control of Maserati from De Tomaso.

This sale was yet another turning point in Maserati's complicated history. It resulted in the introduction of the fourth series of the Quattroporte. Designed by Marcello Gandini, this was the first Maserati that offered **antilock brakes** and airbags.

Forward thinking

Designer Marcello Gandini is remembered for creating some of the most revolutionary supercars in the automotive world. His work included designs for Lamborghini, BMW, and Alfa Romeo. Gandini is credited with popularizing the "wedge" shape of many sports cars from his era and beyond.

Chapter 4

Turning Things Around ⟫ ⟫⟫⟫

Maserati reached the final leg of its climb back from the bottom in 1997. Ferrari—which is now owned by Fiat—took the reigns at Maserati. This was an exciting new era for the company. At Maserati's home in Modena, a state-of-the-art assembly line was installed on the production floor. This was a huge remodeling of the decades-old facility.

Under new management

There were also big things happening at the corporate level. The entire company was given an overhaul. This included the much-anticipated announcement that Maserati cars would be returning to North American markets.

The first release under the new management was the 1998 3200 GT. This streamlined coupe was created by ItalDesign, which had been founded by Maserati designer Giorgetto Giugiaro.

3200 GT

Production years: 1998–2001
No. built: 4,795 (all versions)
Top speed: 174 mph (280 km/h)
Engine type: 90-degree V8
Engine size: 3217 cc (3.2 liters),
   370 hp
Cylinders: 8
Transmission: 6-speed manual
CO_2 emissions: N/A
EPA fuel economy ratings: N/A
Price: N/A

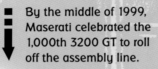 By the middle of 1999,
Maserati celebrated the
1,000th 3200 GT to roll
off the assembly line.

Quattroporte evolution

Maserati's Quattroporte Evoluzione also
came out in 1998. It had a considerable
facelift from the previous Quattroporte—
everything from the stereo to the wheel
rims. It kept the three engine sizes of the
older Quattroporte, though, including
the powerful 3200-cc V8 engine. The
3.2 V8 was the bestselling Quattroporte,
racking up over 800 vehicles produced
between 1998 and 2001.

All the changes and improvements to
the Evoluzione helped the Quattroporte
stand its ground against similar sport
sedans from other companies. It also
helped Maserati climb up to over 2,000
cars produced a year, which was a great
improvement on previous years.

3200 GT Spyder

Sprouted from the popular 3200 GT, the Spyder GT featured a brand new 4.3-liter V8 engine. It also had the new Maserati Info Center in the console. The color display controlled the trip computer as well as the air conditioning and stereo.

The Spyder was more affordable than similar sports cars made by competitors such as Ferrari, coming in at under US$100,000.

Coupe GT

The Spyder version was quickly followed by the Coupe GT version. This dropped much of the 3200 GT's bodywork, including the boomerang-style taillights. With Maserati's return to North America, the 3200 GT was revamped as the 2002 Coupe. It had a more powerful 390 **horsepower (hp)** V8 engine under the hood to appeal to American drivers.

Back to Fiat

In 2005, it was announced that control of Maserati would return to Fiat. The move made for a close working relationship between Maserati and Alfa Romeo, which was also owned by Fiat. Maserati continued to work in cooperation with Ferrari, however. This meant that Maserati was now working alongside two of its former biggest competitors.

Alfa Romeo

Now owned by Fiat, the first Alfa Romeo vehicle was unveiled in 1910. The stylish, four-cylinder, four-liter open-top car had an impressive top speed of almost 62 mph (100 km/h). This marked the beginning of the Italian automaker's legacy of speed and style. Fiats have even appeared on the big screen, driven by fictional super spy James Bond.

Vital Statistics

GranTurismo

Production years: 2007–present
No. built: N/A
Top speed: 177 mph (284 km/h)
Engine type: V90 degree
Engine size: 4244 cc (4.2 liters), 405 hp
Cylinders: 8
Transmission: ZF 6-speed automatic
CO_2 emissions: N/A
EPA fuel economy ratings: 13 mpg (city); 20 mpg (highway)
Price: US$428,000

Première Mondiale

Grand plans

Hot on the heels of this announcement was the release of the Maserati GranTurismo. Thanks once again to designer Pininfarina, the GranTurismo was a nod to Maserati's history—with

 The GranTurismo line included GranTurismo S, MC, and S Automatic versions.

a modern twist. It had a top speed of 177 mph (284 km/h), with a 405-hp, 4.2-liter V8 engine.

Chapter 5
Tearing Up the Track

Maserati's success on the track stretches back decades. It began with Carlo Maserati's first work on motorizing bicycles, and has continued right up to the speeding giants that can be seen on the international raceways of today. Maserati has earned victories at every major racing event around the world.

Ten Tipo 26 racers were built during its production run of two years.

The early years—Tipo 26

Alfieri's Tipo 26 was based on a Grand Prix design he had worked on for Diatto. It won at the 1926 Targa Florio, then again the following year at the Tripoli Grand Prix. The inline eight-cylinder engine had twin overhead **camshafts** and could produce 128 bhp.

Taking the 26B to victory

The next version was the Tipo 26B. It took to the track at the Targa Florio, coming home in third place with Alfieri behind the wheel. It was in a Tipo 26B that Alfieri had a terrible accident while racing in the Messina Cup. Injuries from the crash sidelined Alfieri for some time. In fact, it was these injuries that later

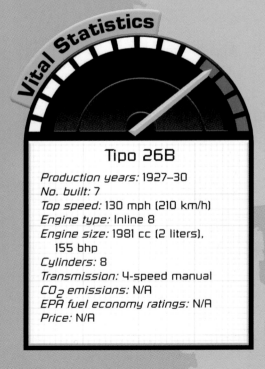

Taken too soon

Carlo Maserati was the man who helped create the Maserati legacy. The eldest brother, it was Carlo whose work with Isotta Fraschini helped his younger siblings enter the automotive world. Sadly, Carlo passed away in 1910, before he was 30 years old. Carlo never saw the success of the company he helped inspire.

resulted in Alfieri's death following surgery five years later. But at the time, Alfieri recovered enough to return with the Tipo 26B to win the Italian Constructors' Championship.

Vital Statistics

Tipo 26B

Production years: 1927–30
No. built: 7
Top speed: 130 mph (210 km/h)
Engine type: Inline 8
Engine size: 1981 cc (2 liters), 155 bhp
Cylinders: 8
Transmission: 4-speed manual
CO_2 emissions: N/A
EPA fuel economy ratings: N/A
Price: N/A

The Tipo V4

The 16-cylinder engine in the Tipo V4 was a combination of two Tipo 26B inline 8 engines. In 1929, the Maserati Tipo V4 set a world speed record of 153 mph (246 km/h). This impressive feat remained the record for eight years, until driver Sir Malcolm Campbell beat it driving a **modified** Bluebird. The Tipo V4 won the Tripoli Grand Prix in 1930 and the Rome Grand Prix in 1931.

26M

Production years: 1930–32
No. built: 13
Top speed: 143 mph (230 km/h)
Engine type: Inline 8
Engine size: 2495 cc (2.5 liters), 240 bhp
Cylinders: 8
Transmission: 4-speed manual
CO_2 emissions: N/A
EPA fuel economy ratings: N/A
Price: N/A

Ernesto Maserati tunes up his V4 before the 1931 Rome Grand Prix. The V4 was a whale of a racer, with a weight of almost 2,315 lb (1,050 kg).

The 26M

The monstrous V4 was followed by the 26M in 1930. It won at the Acerbo Cup and the Tripoli Grand Prix in its first year. Also known as the 8C 2500, the 26M was a big departure from the earlier Tipo 26B. Alfieri had created a new 2.5-liter, 2495-cc engine. The single-seater had a top speed of 143 mph (230 km/h). It earned victories at the Rome, Spain, and Monza Grands Prix in 1930, and again at Monza in 1931. Maserati also came out with a road version of the 26M in 1931. By the time production ended in 1932, 13 of the 26Ms had been produced.

Record-setting driver

Driver Baconin Borzacchini was behind the wheel when the V4 set a speed record of over 153 mph (246 km/h) in 1929. The following year it was Borzacchini who took the Maserati V4 to its first Grand Prix win in Tripoli. He was also one of the last drivers to compete in the Tipo 8C 3000, Maserati's last two-seater Grand Prix car.

The 8CM

Like most Maserati racers, the 8CM underwent several changes and improvements over its lifetime. Begun in 1933, the 8CM was a single-seater with a top speed of almost 155 mph (250 km/h). The chassis for the car was influenced by the 4CM 1100, but designers soon realized the frame was not sturdy enough. While the car's light weight helped with speed, the relatively flimsy frame made control of the 8CM difficult. Eventually, it was made more rigid, and the 8CM went on to win the Belgian and Nice Grands Prix.

The 8CM had a three-liter, eight-cylinder engine.

The 4CTR and beyond

The 4CTR, Alfieri Maserati's last design before his death, was a four-cylinder, 1.1-liter turbocharged racer. It had better control than its predecessor, the 26M. Although this model was shortlived, it paved the way for the Tipo 4CM series. The first 4CM in the series was the 4CM 1100, which was produced from 1932 to 1937.

The single-seater was based heavily on the 4CTR, with the addition of **hydraulic** brakes and improvements to the control system. The 4CM took third place at the 1932 Grand Prix in Nurburgring. The 4CM series went on to include the 1500, 2000, and 2500 models.

The 4CM 1500

The 4CM 1500 proved to be popular outside Italy, helping spread the Maserati name across the rest of Europe. Many drivers praised its handling almost as much as its speed. It went up against powerful racers such as the new eight-cylinder by French automaker Delage. The 4CM 1500 brought home a victory at Nurburgring in 1934, and continued to compete until 1938.

The Tipo 4CM 1100 was produced between 1932 to 1938.

Tripoli Grand Prix

The Tripoli Grand Prix was first held in 1925. Its beginnings were modest, with just nine cars competing on a 132-mile (213-km) circuit. It continued to grow in size and length as the years went on. The last Tripoli Grand Prix was held in 1940, when Italy had joined in the fighting of World War II.

Tipo 4CM 2500

Production years: 1934
No. built: 1
Top speed: 137 mph (220 km/h)
Engine type: Inline 4
Engine size: 2482 cc (2.5 liters), 195 bhp
Cylinders: 4
Transmission: 4-speed manual
CO_2 emissions: N/A
EPA fuel economy ratings: N/A
Price: N/A

Only one of the Tipo 4CM 2000 was made, as with the 4CM 2500.

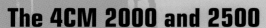

The 4CM 2000 and 2500

A new four-cylinder engine was built into the 4CM 2000. It was a single-seater car, with the steering wheel placed slightly off-center on the dashboard. Unveiled in 1933, the 4CM 2000 had a top speed of 133 mph (215 km/h). The 1934 2500 model came in both a sport and single-seat version. While the body design was shortlived, the 136 mph (220 km/h) engine was later used in other cars.

43

Maserati's competition

The early 1930s were a great time for Maserati on the racetrack. Alfieri and Maserati team drivers enjoyed success with the Tipo 26 and other early models. However, after a good run early in the decade, Maserati found itself facing stiff competition from other European automakers. Ferrari and Alfa Romeo were Maserati's main racing opponents to begin with, but soon German companies such as Daimler-Benz and Auto Union stepped things up.

A change of plan

Bringing home victories on the track is essential for a racing company to survive. Wins at world competitions not only improve an automaker's reputation, but also increase customer interest in the brand. As World War II loomed, Maserati decided to branch out from its Grand Prix efforts into other races. This meant building a new 1.5-liter car.

The Tipo 8CTF had a top speed of almost 180 mph (290 km/h).

The Tipo 8CTF

The Tipo 8CTF was designed by Ernesto Maserati in 1938. Its development would not have been possible without the Maserati brothers selling control of the company to Adolfo Orsi. With the increase in finances, Ernesto was able to put a three-liter, supercharged engine under the hood. The car made its first track appearance in 1938 at the Grand Prix in Tripoli, with less-than-impressive results.

The onset of World War II was also an obstacle to the development of the 8CTF, as the number of potential races was limited. Nonetheless, the 8CTF eventually prevailed, winning the famous Indianapolis 500 in 1939 and 1940. This was the first time an Italian car had won the race.

Vital Statistics

8CTF

Production years: 1938–39
No. built: N/A
Top speed: 177 mph (285 km/h)
Engine type: Vertical inline 8
Engine size: 2991 cc (3 liters),
   366 bhp
Cylinders: 8
Transmission: 4-speed manual
CO_2 emissions: N/A
EPA fuel economy ratings: N/A
Price: N/A

⟫⟫ Hydraulics

In 1933, Maserati became one of the first automakers to produce cars that included hydraulic brakes. Hydraulic brakes use moving liquids under pressure to operate the brake pads that slow the tires of a vehicle. This pressure is controlled by the brake pedal. The harder you push on the pedal, the more the fluids are compressed, which increases the amount of friction of the brake pads against the wheels.

Maserati's braking first

Maserati saw the advantages of hydraulic brakes over the traditional mechanical brake system, which involved a system of cables and pulleys. This older style was hard to maintain and prone to malfunctioning. Maserati adopted hydraulic brakes before other auto manufacturers.

The hydraulic brake system was introduced to the 8C and 8CM in 1933.

46

The last brothers' Maserati

The final racecar designed by the Maserati brothers was the A6G CS in 1947. The car featured a new natural aspiration engine. This means that air is pulled into the cylinder naturally, instead of being forced into it mechanically as with a supercharged engine.

The A6G CS engine was a two-liter with 130 bhp. It came in single- and two-seater models. Only 15 of the A6G CS were made, with most sold to racers in Brazil. In 1947 and 1948, the Maserati A6G CS won the Italian Championship.

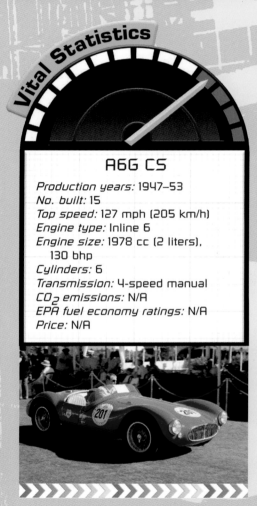

Vital Statistics

A6G CS

Production years: 1947–53
No. built: 15
Top speed: 127 mph (205 km/h)
Engine type: Inline 6
Engine size: 1978 cc (2 liters), 130 bhp
Cylinders: 6
Transmission: 4-speed manual
CO$_2$ emissions: N/A
EPA fuel economy ratings: N/A
Price: N/A

The A6G CS came in one- and two-seater models; the two-seater competed in Formula 2 races.

 Maserati built 60 of the A6G CS/54 during its production run.

Different strokes

Another first for Maserati was the A6G CS/53 in 1953. This was the first Maserati with a short-stroke engine. In previous racers, the pistons were larger, which made for more movement inside the cylinder, especially at high speeds. The short-stroke engine had smaller pistons, which could produce the same high speeds with less wear on the engine.

The A6G in the 1950s

The A6G CS/53 had a top speed of 146 mph (235 km/h). It won at the Italian Championships in 1953 and 1954. It also took first at the 1954 Targa Florio, Giro di Sicilia, and Irish Tourist Trophy. The Maserati A6G/54, also known as the 2000 Gran Turismo, proved to be more

popular than the 1953 model. Maserati offered the car in several design options, including coupe and spyder versions. It brought home a victory at the 1956 Italian Championship.

Italian competition

The racing giant Ferrari was founded in 1947 by Enzo Ferrari. The Italian automaker produces sports cars as well as powerful racing cars. Ferrari is known for speed as well as comfort and control. The company logo is a black horse on a yellow background, which celebrates the company's birthplace of Modena, Italy.

New rules

In 1954, the engine rules for Formula 1 racing changed to 2.5 liters, which meant that Maserati had to come up with a new vehicle in order to compete, and especially to take on its biggest competitor, Ferrari. The result was the Maserati 250F. Great efforts were made to improve weight distribution and engine power, but unfortunately the 250F experienced several setbacks, including production delays and engine trouble.

The 250F on the track

The 250F had a top speed of 180 mph (290 km/h) with an impressive 220 bhp. Between 1954 and 1957, the 250F earned eight Grand Prix victories. It even scored a first at the 1957 Formula 1 World Championship. The 250F was also the car driven by the first female driver to compete at Formula 1 level. A 12-cylinder version was made in 1957, but this was abandoned when Maserati retired from team racing later that year.

Vital Statistics

250F T2

Production years: 1957
No. built: 3
Top speed: 189 mph (305 km/h)
Engine type: 60-degree V12
Engine size: 2490 cc (2.5 liters), 300 bhp
Cylinders: 12
Transmission: 5-speed manual
CO_2 emissions: N/A
EPA fuel economy ratings: N/A
Price: N/A

A Maserati 250F (car number 34) speeds past a Ferrari crash at the 1957 Monaco Grand Prix.

A legendary racer

One of the most powerful cars of its generation, the 450S had a tremendous opening season in 1957. The short-stroke, 4.5-liter V8 either won or retired in each of its races that year. This included a win at the 1957 Formula 1 championship. The 450S was known for its very loud engine, and had a top speed of almost 200 mph (320 km/h). The engine had initially been designed to compete in the North American Indianapolis 500.

Operation Fangio

The 450S also had a colorful history off the track. In 1958, the 450S was due to compete in the Cuban Grand Prix. But the night before the race Cuban revolutionaries kidnapped the driver, Juan Manuel Fangio, and held him for ransom. Fangio was eventually released unharmed, but he was kept from competing in the race. A movie was made about his experience in 1999, called *Operation Fangio*.

Modifying the 450S

After its withdrawal from team racing in 1957, Maserati still had many of the 450S engines left over, so the V8 engine of the 450S was combined with the 3500 GT to make the 5000 GT in 1959. Some modifications had to be made to the monster engine to allow it to fit on the frame, but despite this, the 450S engine

The Indy 500

The Indianapolis 500 has been held each year on Memorial Day weekend since 1911. Drivers face a grueling 500-mile (804-km) endurance race. Today, the Indianapolis Motor Speedway welcomes crowds of over 500,000 people for the event, with millions more watching on television at home.

still kept most of its racing power. This made for some incredibly fast road cars, reaching speeds of up to 170 mph (273 km/h). The cars were so powerful, in fact, that the company warned potential owners about the dangers of exceeding the speed limits on public roadways.

- Between 1957 and 1962, the 450S earned over 30 victories. It was a favorite to win the coveted World Sports Car Championship in 1957, but car troubles and other problems got in the way.

Vital Statistics

450S

Production years: 1956–58
No. built: 10
Top speed: 200 mph (320 km/h)
Engine type: 90 degree V8
Engine size: 4477.9 cc (4.5 liters), 400 bhp
Cylinders: 8
Transmission: 5-speed manual
CO_2 emissions: N/A
EPA fuel economy ratings: N/A
Price: N/A

≫≫ Fast and reliable

The 300S debuted in 1956, and it quickly became known for its solid handling and speed. A durable racer, the 300S model had a long lifespan. Almost 30 years after production began, 19 of the 29 cars were still driving.

The 300S won the 1,000-km race at Nurburgring in 1956. It also took first at the 1956 Venezuelan Grand Prix, the Australian Tourist Trophy, and the Nassau Trophy. In 1957, the 300S won the Cuban, Sao Paulo, and Lisbon Grands Prix. Its engine would be used to help design the roadgoing Maserati 3500 GT in 1957.

The 300S had a top speed of 180 mph (289 km/h).

The Tipo 61 was basically a Birdcage but with a bigger engine.

Vital Statistics

300S

Production years: 1956–58
No. built: 29
Top speed: 180 mph (289 km/h)
Engine type: Inline 6
Engine size: 2992 cc (3 liters), 245 bhp
Cylinders: 6
Transmission: 4-speed manual
CO_2 emissions: N/A
EPA fuel economy ratings: N/A
Price: N/A

Lightweight and speedy

The Tipo 61's larger engine allowed it to compete in North American racing as well as European competitions. Its lightweight frame also gave it a competitive edge in terms of speed. The Tipo 61 came first in its class at the SCCA Championships in 1960 and 1961. It also won the Cuban Grand Prix in 1960 and the 1961 Four Hours of Rouen in France. The Tipo 61 is considered by many to be one of the best when it comes to front-engine placement racecars.

AMAZING FACTS

Maserati in the U.S.A.

Of the 16 Tipo 61 cars made, not a single one stayed in Europe—all of them went to customers in the United States. Many would undergo drastic design alterations by their owners before entering competitions.

Back to the track

After a long time away from the track, Maserati made its return to racing in the 1990s. One of its first contenders was the Ghibli Open Cup in 1995. The car was based on the two-liter Ghibli road model. The engine was given more power to compete on the racetrack. There was also the addition of a rollcage, racing seat, and fire-suppression system.

Vital Statistics

Ghibli Open Cup

Production years: 1993
No. built: 22
Top speed: 164 mph (263 km/h)
Engine type: 90-degree V6
Engine size: 1996 cc (2 liters),
   320 bhp
Cylinders: 6
Transmission: 6-speed manual
CO_2 emissions: N/A
EPA fuel economy ratings: N/A
Price: US$84,432 (1995)

■ The MC12 bore a passing resemblance to Ferrari's Enzo model, but it had many changes, including a longer wheelbase.

The Trofeo's extremely powerful engine was boosted by 38 bhp, bringing it up to a whopping 488 bhp.

Taking the lead

The release of the MC12 was the next big step in Maserati's return to racing. Launched in 2004, the MC12 competed in that year's FIA GT GT2 class races. The powerful newcomer came second and third, as well as bringing home a victory. In 2005, the MC12 won the FIA GT Manufacturers' Cup. Made under control of Ferrari, the Maserati MC12 can reach 205 mph (330 km/h).

Maserati racing today

The GranTurismo MC Trofeo's roots can be found in the GranTurismo S road model. Development of the GranTurismo S evolved into the GranTurismo MC concept car. This prototype eventually led to the creation of the GranTurismo MC Trofeo in 2010. Even though the car is still in its infancy, it has already undergone some significant changes.

The FIA

The Federation Internationale de l'Automobile (FIA) governs competitive motor sports. Founded in 1904, the FIA controls 227 organizations around the world. This includes Formula 1, World Rally, and World Touring championships. The FIA also publishes a magazine called "InMotion," keeping readers informed about developments in the FIA network.

Chapter 6

Maserati Today and Tomorrow

Few companies have survived as many setbacks as Maserati. It has weathered war, several ownership changes, and even the threat of liquidation. Through all of this, the Italian automotive icon has not only survived, but thrived. The evidence of this can be seen in Maserati's lineup of modern road vehicles.

The GranTurismo's engine has a maximum power output of 405 bhp and a top speed of 178 mph (286 km/h).

The GranTurismo

The GranTurismo is a modern coupe that seats four. Unveiled in 2007, it incorporates ideas from the classic 1947 A6 GranTurismo and the Birdcage. This includes the traditional air vents set behind the front wheels. It was joined by the Sport version in 2008 and a convertible in 2012.

The GranCabrio

The GranCabrio is a four-seater version of the popular GranTurismo S, and is the first drop-top in the company's history. It was created by a new initiative at the company to change the way the driving public views a **cabriolet**. Unveiled in 2009, its engine is an eight-cylinder, 4691-cc, V90 degree with 440 bhp.

Pininfarina

Founded in 1930 by Battista Pininfarina, the Italian design firm quickly developed a reputation for building quality road vehicles. One of their earliest designs, the 1946 Cisitalia, is on display at the Museum of Modern Art. Pininfarina has worked with Ferrari, Alfa Romeo, Fiat, and General Motors.

Vital Statistics

Quattroporte

Production years: 2004–present
No. built: Still in production
Top speed: 167 mph (270 km/h)
Engine type: V90 degree
Engine size: 4244 cc (4.2 liters), 40 bhp
Cylinders: 8
Transmission: Automatic
CO_2 emissions: 345 g/km
EPA fuel economy ratings: 12 mpg (city); 20 mpg (highway)
Price: US$134,700

The Quattroporte today

Also designed by Pininfarina, the latest Quattroporte has received high praise from drivers and the media alike for its blend of new features, comfort, and speed.

The new Quattroporte is heavier than its modern-day counterparts, but still offers a top speed of 167 mph (270 km/h). The weight distribution layout contributes to the Quattroporte V's excellent handling. The engine is set behind the front axle to move the weight toward the rear of the car.

The Quattroporte comes in the standard, Sport GT, Sport GTS (pictured), and Executive GT.

The home of Maserati in Modena, Italy.

The Modena factory today

Maserati has called Modena in Italy its home since 1940. Several expansions have taken place at the factory head-quarters, growing out and around from the original brick building. There is now a modern tower of offices as well as a Maserati showroom for visiting guests. The Modena operation is almost 52,000 square feet and employees 300 people.

There are over 26 workstations. The plant also includes testing areas for engines and cars before they leave the factory. Today's Maserati assembly line includes much more machinery than it did in the past. However, the engines in the Quattroporte and GranTurismo are hand-built and assembled at Ferrari's Maranello headquarters.

Looking ahead

Adapting to the auto market of the day is one of the main reasons Maserati has been able to stay in business for so many years. This has made for dozens of "firsts" for the company, everything from engine power to additional passenger seating. In 2011 Maserati announced its latest evolution—the creation of the very first Maserati Sport Utility Vehicle (SUV).

The SUV

The Sport Utility Vehicle began to grow in popularity in the 1980s. The vehicles were based on trucks, with similar four-wheel drive and strong body frames. Early SUVs were meant for off-road driving on rough terrain. They slowly evolved for regular road driving, with more emphasis put on comfort and style.

■ Designed by Giugiaro, the Kubang is reported to have a 4.2-liter, V8 engine, with a top speed of almost 159 mph (256 km/h).

The Maserati Kubang was unveiled at the 2011 Frankfurt Auto Show. The move into the SUV market was a huge leap for the automaker, not to mention a bit of a gamble, since other larger companies have been making them for years. The idea has been in the works since 2003, when design plans were shown at the Detroit Auto Show. It is still in the "concept" stage of development.

Maserati Timeline

1908	Alfieri Maserati wins his first Grand Prix
1914	Maserati automakers is founded
1926	The first all-Maserati racer, the Tipo 26, is produced
1929	The Tipo V4 sets a world speed record of 153 mph (246 km/h)
1930	The 8C 2500 is launched as a road and racecar
1932	Alfieri Maserati dies
1933	Work begins on the 8CM
1939	Maserati moves from Bologna to Modena; World War II begins
1940	The 8CTF wins the Indianapolis 500
1947	The A6 1500 is unveiled at the Geneva Motor Show; the Maserati brothers leave the company
1952	Gioacchino Colombo becomes Maserati's chief designer
1953	The A6G CS/53 is the first Maserati with a short-stroke engine
1954	The first 250F is produced
1957	The 250F takes four wins on the Grand Prix circuit
1959	The 3500 GT becomes Maserati's first exclusively road vehicle
1960	The Birdcage (Tipo 60) is launched
1963	Production begins on the Sebring and Mistral models
1968	The Orsi group sells Maserati to Citroën
1969	The last of the first Quattroportes is produced
1971	Launch of the first Maserati mid-engine, the Bora
1972	The Merak is unveiled
1973	Yom Kippur War leads to worldwide oil crisis
1974	The Quattroporte series is revived with the Quattroporte II
1975	Citroën leaves Maserati; Alejandro De Tomaso takes over
1977	The Kyalami 4.2 is released
1978	The Quattroporte III sees the first real success for the series
1981	The Biturbo first series is released
1993	Fiat takes over Maserati
1997	Ferrari takes control at Maserati
1998	The 3200 GT and Quattroporte Evoluzione are launched
1999	The 1,000th 3200 GT rolls off the production line
2004	The newly launched MC12 proves itself on the racetrack
2005	Control of Maserati returns to Fiat
2007	The first GranTurismo is produced
2010	The GranTurismo MC Trofeo is born
2011	The first Maserati SUV is announced

Further Information

Books

Maserati
by Martin Buckley
(Haynes Publishing, 2011)

Maseratis (Wild Wheels)
by Bob Power
(Gareth Stevens, 2011)

Maserati (Ultimate Cars)
by Jill C. Wheeler
(ABDO, 2004)

Websites

www.maserati.com/
The official Maserati website.

www.maseratinet.com/
The largest online club for Maserati fans.

www.maserati.com/maserati/en/en/index/maseraticorse.html
The home page of the Trofeo Maserati GranTurismo MC series.

Glossary

antilock brakes A braking system that stops cars quickly on slippery surfaces by improving traction

automatic transmission A device that shifts a car's gears without help from the driver according to the speed it is traveling

brake horsepower (bhp) The raw horsepower of an engine before the loss of power caused by the alternator, gearbox, differential, pumps, etc.

cabriolet A car with a folding top

camshaft A rod in a car's engine; as the camshaft turns, it pushes the pistons up and down, compressing gas in the engine and powering the car

chassis The strong support structure that connects the engine to the wheels and holds the body to the car

concept car A vehicle made to show the public a new design or technology

coupe A hard-topped sports car with two doors

cylinder The chamber in an engine in which the piston moves

cylinder blocks The part of a car that contains the piston chambers

embargo A governmental law that does not allow trade with a specific country

grand tourer A two-seater sports car that is made for driving long distances

horsepower (hp) The amount of pulling power an engine has based on the number of horses it would take to pull the same load

hydraulic Something that is powered or operated by water

iconic Something that is much loved and admired

industrialist Someone who owns or is the director of a large industrial company

liquidating Dissolving a company so that it no longer exists

longevity A long life; lasting a long time

manual transmission A device that a driver must operate to shift a car's gears

modified When something is altered so that it suits a particular purpose

production cars Cars that are made in large numbers on an assembly line

sedan A passenger car with four doors and a back seat

spark plugs The parts of a car's cylinder head that ignite the fuel

spyder An open-topped two-seater car

supercharged When an air compressor is used for the forced induction of an internal combustion engine

suspension A system of springs that protects the chassis of a car

turbochargers Gas compressors in the engine that make a vehicle go faster

Index

Entries in **bold** indicate pictures